WE ARE AMONG US

Stephen Belber

BROADWAY PLAY PUBLISHING INC
New York
www.broadwayplaypub.com
info@broadwayplaypub.com

First edition: May 2022
I S B N: 978-0-88145-923-4

Book design: Marie Donovan
Page make-up: Adobe InDesign
Typeface: Palatino

WE ARE AMONG US was first produced by City Theatre, Pittsburgh, running from 11 May-2 June 2019. The cast and creative contributors were:

KHADIJA .... Nilanjana Bose
TAYLOR.. Kyle Haden
SHAR .... Jo Mei
LAURA .... Lisa Velten Smith
BEAU ....Eric Wiegand

Director .... Adrienne Campbell-Holt
Scenic Designer ....Narelle Sissons
Costume Designer....................................... Sarita P Fellows
Lighting Designer....................... Andrew David Ostrowski
Sound Designer ....Zachary Beattie-Brown
Production Stage Manager .... Patti Kelly

CHARACTERS

KHADIJA, 26, *Afghan but fairly Americanized; a lotta life*
LAURA, 40s, *White; former army reserves; strong,
   thoughtful*
SHAR, 30s, *Vietnamese, female; intense/imperfect conviction*
BEAU, 21, LAURA's *son; smart, lost, wants to figure it out*
TAYLOR, 40, *Black; former Army Special Forces, now a cop*

All actors remain on stage for the duration

(KHADIJA, 26, *stands in light and speaks to us*)

KHADIJA: *(Eyes closed)* What it feels like. *Right now.* In Kabul, Afghanistan, on a dusty-crowded street in the middle of July with the sun beating down and people just trying to survive. *(Eyes open)* I'm on the outskirts of the city and what I see are car parts; millions of them; rusted and dirty, oily and corroded. Car parts and *men*; in Pakol caps and grey turbans, staring at me as I try not to stare back, their eyes glinting sadness and horror that I am wearing a hijab but not a khima, even though *they're* the ones who should be averting their eyes. Elsewhere are thousands of *wheelbarrows*, overloaded with wrapped parcels or aging bananas or bottles of Sprite or pipe connectors or tiny soap bars or grain sacks or floor cushions or rubber tires that seem to have travelled the world twice over. And there are pale blue-burqa'd women who pass me and I can't tell if they're judging or admiring but either way I feel immense love for each and every one of them. *(Pause)* Just south of the city is our famous mountain, T V Hill, crammed with towering antennas staring stoically down, sending their electromagnetic messages of love and hate and prayer and propaganda and truth and bullshit. *(Pause)* Which for a moment makes me think of America. Of what it feels like, right now, in La Jolla California, of all the places, my home away from home. In the parking lot outside of Rubio's, the semi-fast-food, semi-Mexican place with its super burritos and chip bar and steady stream of teenagers endlessly refilling their soda cups. ...They *too* are trying to survive. *(Beat)* I close my eyes and I am standing with them. *(Eyes closed)* This is what it feels like. At this moment. Right here in La Jolla. *(She opens her eyes)* "An Afghan girl in *these* United States."

(Lights shift)

*(*BEAU *and* LAURA *coexist; they eat Vanilla Swiss Almond...)*

LAURA: How was work?

BEAU: Dumb.

LAURA: Why? *(She waits.)* Beau?

BEAU: Mom?

LAURA: Why?

BEAU: I dunno. ...I think I'm done with that job.

LAURA: You've been saying that for six months.

BEAU: Well now I mean it.

LAURA: Good. Animal lovers shouldn't work at pet stores.

BEAU: I'm not an animal lover.

LAURA: Well, you *like* animals—

BEAU: I like *mice*.

LAURA: You sell *mice*?

BEAU: Mice are popular.

LAURA: Either way you could find a better job—

BEAU: It's just until I—

LAURA: —even if it's just until you go back to school.

BEAU: You're saying this 'cause you want me to make more—

LAURA: That's *not true*—

BEAU: —so that I move out—

LAURA: It's *not true*—

BEAU: It's not?—

LAURA: I *love* having you here, I just want you to be happy—

BEAU: I'm happy—

LAURA: You're happy?—

BEAU: I'm happy—

LAURA: Well then that's all I want. …I just don't think that selling pets and playing incessant *Assassin's Creed* is a pathway to—

BEAU: "Incessant *Assassin's Creed*"?—

LAURA: Fine— "*Incessantly* playing *Assassin's Creed*"—

BEAU: —is that really where you wanna go? —After my *beloved video games*?

LAURA: *(A smile)* No.

BEAU: …I sometimes think Margo flushes the mice.

LAURA: That's sadistic.

BEAU: Yeah—

LAURA: Why on *earth* would Margo flush—?

BEAU: Not every mouse is popular, some are just—

LAURA: Ugly?

BEAU: Unloved.

LAURA: What creates an unloved mouse? *Personality?*

BEAU: I don't know.

LAURA: Is it that they're not mousey enough? Do people want more *mousey* mice?

BEAU: That's really cool, Mom.

LAURA: Am I being too silly?

BEAU: A touch.

(LAURA *looks at* BEAU, *a genuine smile…*)

BEAU: Wanna see that movie after work tomorrow?

LAURA: I actually have something at five.

BEAU: You "have" something?

LAURA: I do.

BEAU: What do you have?

LAURA: An interview.

BEAU: For a job?

LAURA: No.

BEAU: Why not?

LAURA: Why don't I have a *job* interview?—

BEAU: Yeah—

LAURA: 'Cause I like my job—

BEAU: Do you?

LAURA: Mostly—

BEAU: Want me to grab you a pet store application?

LAURA: No I don't want that—

BEAU: Ten seventy-five an hour—all the mice you can eat—

LAURA: I'm good, thanks.

(BEAU *shrugs; beat*)

BEAU: I started that book you recommended.

LAURA: It's not a book, Beau, it's an essay.

BEAU: Well it's a long-ass essay.

LAURA: Are you liking it?

BEAU: I actually am.

LAURA: Good. I think it says a lot about who we are as a country.

BEAU: Mom.

LAURA: Beau—

BEAU: Don't try and make it something it's not.

LAURA: I'm not—

BEAU: You are—

LAURA: I'm saying it gave me a fresh perspective on people who come from different backgrounds—

BEAU: Oh please—

LAURA: Oh please what?—

BEAU: Oh please we shouldn't need a book to tell us what it's like to be poor—

LAURA: Well how else are we supposed to—?

BEAU: Just go be poor for a while, it frickin' sucks—

LAURA: When have you been poor?—

BEAU: Well I'm certainly not rich.

LAURA: Exactly, you sell fucking mice—

BEAU: Exactly—

LAURA: *Exactly. (Beat)* Will you try to *finish* the essay?

BEAU: Yes, Mother, I'll try my darnedest to "finish" the essay.

LAURA: I'm just saying—

BEAU: It's not like I don't have the *mental rigor* to finish an *essay*, I'm just at a point in my life where I *arduously* believe that life experience trumps *books*. Whereas people who sit around "reading" all day are somehow able to convince themselves that they're living when in fact they're just getting *gradually fat and gross*.

LAURA: As opposed to the "arduousness" of virtual reality, which keeps you "svelte"?

BEAU: I'm not svelte because of virtual reality, *Jane Fonda*, it's because I do sit-ups.

LAURA: Is that right?

BEAU: Yeah, like fifty every day. It's exhausting.

LAURA: I've never see you do fifty sit-ups, Beau.

BEAU: Mom, I did fifty sit-ups this morning.

LAURA: You sure they were sit-*ups*?

BEAU: ...What is that? Are you trying to be funny?

LAURA: No, but I know you and thus I know that a sit-up for *you* is probably more like a slouch-*down*.

BEAU: Oh my God, you *are* trying to be funny—

LAURA: It's just an observation.

BEAU: Is this the result of some sort of *adult night* class for stand-up comedy?

LAURA: *Beau*—

BEAU: *Mom*—

LAURA: Beau—

BEAU: Mom.

LAURA: Do you know...

BEAU: How much you love me?

LAURA: Yeah.

BEAU: ...Yes.

(BEAU *and* LAURA *stand in silence...*)

(*Lights shift suddenly*—)

(SHAR *with* LAURA—)

SHAR: Northern Virginia!

LAURA: It is what it is.

SHAR: You like it?

LAURA: Not really.

SHAR: Yeah—lotta Rite-Aids. So—thanks for doing this. I know it's been some time.

LAURA: It has.

SHAR: And that it's often easier to just push on, so I appreciate you agreeing to meet.

(LAURA nods a little)

SHAR: As I said on the phone, I'm a free-lance reporter but this'll be a *Harper's* article about Roger Hawkins running for mayor of Wilmington, Delaware.

LAURA: Right.

SHAR: I actually reported in Afghanistan, Wardak Province, 2009 to 2011—

LAURA: Yeah, I saw that.

SHAR: During which time I heard about the Haroun case. So in addition to writing about the campaign, I'd also like to ask a bit about that.

LAURA: Like I said, I can only speak to him as a person. I don't have information on particular events—

SHAR: Absolutely—

LAURA: —even though I imagine it's what you're looking for, but the fact is I just don't, you probably know more than I do.

SHAR: Well let's just go through it once more?

LAURA: ...Okay.

SHAR: *(A smile)* Okay—so—in terms of you: College army reserves, did your eight years while working for an ad firm in Seattle. Curious what made you sign up.

LAURA: I believe people should contribute.

SHAR: Of course—so then in 2008 you left the ad job and joined *G S Risk Management,* which had a two year Pentagon contract for "Defense Reutilization and Marketing"?

LAURA: That's right—

SHAR: Which means—?

LAURA: Surplus property reuse, transfer and disposal.

SHAR: So you—supplied furniture?

LAURA: Furniture, tents, trucks, weapons.

SHAR: Good money?

LAURA: That's not why I did it.

SHAR: Gotcha. So—on December 16, 2009, you were at Outpost Sanchez helping resupply a unit that was conducting "village stability" operations?

LAURA: Yep—

SHAR: And Abdul-Jalil Haroun was brought in for questioning at seven P M by Delta Force operators Jack Billings, Taylor McGinnis and Roger Hawkins, who then claimed to have released him the next morning at six, which you didn't personally see, but during those eleven hours of detainment you told C I D that you *did* hear some, quote, "noises of pain" coming from the interrogation room.

LAURA: I heard the guy shouting a couple times.

SHAR: And you heard that prior to going to sleep, then once more when you got up to use the latrine?

LAURA: It was nine years ago.

SHAR: Eight—so once more when you went to the latrine?

LAURA: I guess.

SHAR: Gotcha. I know this probably isn't fun, so I do apologize.

LAURA: It's fine.

SHAR: Now as you know, Mr Haroun's body was found three weeks later in an unmarked grave less than a mile from the outpost's second perimeter. He had broken bones, lacerated skin, burn lesions, neck ligatures and other signs likely indicating torture. Would you say you were close to the three soldiers in question?

LAURA: I wouldn't say close.

SHAR: But you were at that outpost fairly often?—

LAURA: You know I have to say it's quite annoying that you misrepresented the topic of this talk.

SHAR: …Well, I *did* say it was about Roger Hawkins running for mayor, no? You didn't think I was gonna ask about what happened that night?—

LAURA: You're coming off a little aggressive.

SHAR: I'm sorry. *(Honest)* I am. How might I better—?

LAURA: I think we should just keep it about the character of Roger Hawkins.

SHAR: Okay, but his character definitely played a role that night. I think?—Yes?

LAURA: *(Deadpan)* Are we gunning for a Pulitzer?

SHAR: Just trying to tell what happened—

LAURA: I stated that I didn't wanna get into—

SHAR: Excuse me, Laura, you're a very smart person, you didn't think I was gonna ask about some of this? A man just won the democratic primary for mayor of a city of seventy-two thousand people, he was once investigated for a war crime, you don't think it's a fair question?—

LAURA: I think Roger Hawkins is a capable leader with a very strong set of skills—

SHAR: Good—so I'm just looking for information concerning—

LAURA: I have information concerning *capable leadership*—

SHAR: —well that's exactly what I'm—

LAURA: —including a Distinguished Service Cross—

SHAR: I'm not talking about—

LAURA: —an Award For Valor and two Purple Hearts, none of which I see hanging off of you.

SHAR: …Is it "off-putting" to you to discuss the—

LAURA: Why would it be off-putting?—

SHAR: Because this is possibly a fraught subject for you due to possible inaccuracies you conveyed to C I D investigators at the time. Which are possibly a significant part of why this case never went to trial and why no one in America has even heard of it. *(Gentle)* I'm gonna write the story anyway, Laura; wouldn't you prefer to have a say?

LAURA: Not if it's driven by agenda—

SHAR: It's *investigative*—

LAURA: Right—

SHAR: You're the only outside witness whose testimony could shed light on a case that would go to trial in any civilian courtroom. Your voice should be in this article—

LAURA: *(Standing)* I think I'm done—

SHAR: I'm just asking if you think Roger Hawkins deserves—

LAURA: No—what you're doing is lacking an objective understanding of what people over there were—

SHAR: *Excuse me— (Calm but steady)* —I saw with my own eyes what people were trying to do, Laura, and most were good and their efforts unquestionably worthy, but it doesn't take a high I Q to know there were some messed up things happening as well— blame it on the individual or the system that *made* those individuals—but there were clearly some fucked up events that I'm merely trying to examine, and quite frankly others are talking to me, so I would think you'd at least want your—

LAURA: You can leave now—

BEAU: Hey— *(Who's caught this last part—)*

LAURA: Jesus—

BEAU: Sorry—

LAURA: You scared me—

BEAU: Sorry.

LAURA: *(To* SHAR*)* …This is my son, Beau.

SHAR: Hi, Beau.

BEAU: Hi.

SHAR: *(Hand extended)* Shar Caskins; I was interviewing your Mom for an article I'm writing.

BEAU: About what?

SHAR: Her time in Afghanistan—

LAURA: Ms Caskins was just leaving.

BEAU: Okay.

SHAR: *(Honest, to* LAURA*)* I'm sorry if you're upset; it wasn't my intention. *(Sunny)* By the way, this is a nice apartment. *(To* BEAU*)* You live here too?

BEAU: I'm saving money for college.

SHAR: Hey, lots of people do it.

BEAU: Do what?

SHAR: Live with their folks—

LAURA: Can you please leave?

(BEAU *takes this in.*)

SHAR: Absolutely. Nice to meet you, Beau. (*Offering her card*) If you'd be open to talking—

LAURA: Goodbye

BEAU: (*To* SHAR) No thanks.

SHAR: Of course. (*She smiles, pockets the card*) Have a good day. (*She leaves*)

(*Silence…*BEAU *studies* LAURA, *who busies herself…*)

BEAU: What was that?

LAURA: She just told you.

BEAU: She seemed like a jerk.

LAURA: She was.

(*More silence as* BEAU *looks at* LAURA… *Then—*)

BEAU: What're the fucked up events. That she was—?

LAURA: I'll tell you later.

(BEAU *just looks at* LAURA.)

LAURA: It's not significant.

BEAU: I'm just—

LAURA: Honestly—can we talk about it later?

(BEAU *absorbs. He looks at* LAURA… *Then—*)

BEAU: Okay, Mom.

LAURA: Thank you.

(*Lights shift*)

(SHAR *and* KHADIJA *at a Mexican fast-food joint*)

SHAR: So this is nice. I mean *La Jolla.*

KHADIJA: I love La Jolla. I thought you meant this place.

SHAR: This is nice too.

KHADIJA: It's called *Rubio's.*

SHAR: Yes I know—

KHADIJA: The food's actually good, and as you can see, it's just across the parking lot from where I work.

SHAR: I didn't mean to show up announced.

KHADIJA: I was due for a break anyway.

SHAR: And is Whole Foods a good place to work?

KHADIJA: It's great; eleven dollars an hour!

SHAR: We could've stayed there.

KHADIJA: I didn't want my colleagues thinking I was in trouble.

SHAR: Because I'm interviewing you?

KHADIJA: Yeah.

SHAR: I can guarantee you're not in trouble.

(KHADIJA smiles, grateful.)

SHAR: I know you didn't want to meet—

KHADIJA: I didn't—

SHAR: And I promise I won't take too much of your time.

(KHADIJA nods.)

SHAR: So do you like it out here?

KHADIJA: I love it. I was in Chattanooga for four years, which, I dunno, it's fine—

SHAR: It sucks—

KHADIJA: Yeah—

SHAR: Which I'm sure sounds elitist, but c'mon, it sucks.

KHADIJA: Well, maybe compared to La Jolla. I mean, the Whole Foods there is not the same as this one.

SHAR: Is that right?—

KHADIJA: This one has a million more things.

SHAR: Like—?

KHADIJA: Like Spirulina, which is a complete protein, which is good if you don't eat meat.

SHAR: Do you eat meat?

KHADIJA: Yes I do, but a lot of the customers out here don't and so I'm able to point them to the spirulina section of the store, or I should say the spirulina *shelf*, which I couldn't do in Tennessee—am I talking too much?

SHAR: Not at all. It's great to meet you. So you live with your aunt out here?

KHADIJA: Yes but she's not really my aunt, she's the aunt of my aunt. In Chattanooga I lived with a cousin but here I live with the aunt of an aunt.

SHAR: And how did you learn such good English?

KHADIJA: Do you think it's good?!—

SHAR: I do—

KHADIJA: I don't, I think about it everyday and I think that after this many years I should be better.

SHAR: Four years isn't that much.

KHADIJA: Four in America, three in Jordan where they taught us almost everyday, and when my family lived in Kabul, I was also able to study it.

SHAR: And so you left Afghanistan—

KHADIJA: When I was eighteen.

SHAR: And when your father died—?

KHADIJA: I was sixteen. And I was fifteen when my mother died.

SHAR: Right.

KHADIJA: I'm not trying to make you feel sorry for me.

SHAR: I'm not—

KHADIJA: Good because this isn't about that, or it shouldn't be because I'm doing just fine.

SHAR: I know, you make eleven bucks an hour.

KHADIJA: And I get to eat all the spirulina I want even though I also eat meat. I am very free.

SHAR: ...And *how* did you mother die?

KHADIJA: She was hit by a military vehicle.

SHAR: An *American* military—?

KHADIJA: Yes. It was an accident.

SHAR: ...What type of vehicle?

KHADIJA: A tank.

SHAR: What happened?

KHADIJA: She was crossing the road, and...I guess she thought it would stop. But by an accident it sped up.

SHAR: ...Did the American government—?

KHADIJA: Yes, they gave my family bereavement money. Ten thousand dollars. It was actually what helped me get to Jordan and live there, and eventually the visa process, which was costly.

SHAR: I assume the U S government knew all this when they processed the application?—

KHADIJA: Very much so.

SHAR: That both your parents died at the hands of Americans? —Under regrettable and questionable circumstances.

KHADIJA: I am sure that's why I'm here.

SHAR: You gotta hand it to 'em.

KHADIJA: They didn't have to. And maybe they did it out of guilt, but I am at least grateful for the gesture. *(And then)* Which is why I don't think I want to participate with your article. Even though you seem very nice. I don't want to hurt the hand that feeds me.

SHAR: Whole Foods is the one that's feeding you, Khadijah.

KHADIJA: It is a very American company.

(SHAR *smiles, nods…beat.*)

SHAR: So do you have a boyfriend?

KHADIJA: *(A big smile)* Do I look like I do?

SHAR: Why, do you look different when you do and when you don't?

KHADIJA: I don't actually know! But yes, I bet you I do.

SHAR: I *totally* look different when I have a boyfriend.

KHADIJA: Do you *glow?*

SHAR: No, I'm more of a *glistener.*

KHADIJA: What is this?

SHAR: I *glisten.* It's more sparkly and twinkly than a glow. A glow is a little more nuanced. A glow is what cool people do. I would bet *you* glow.

KHADIJA: I don't think I glow—

SHAR: I bet you glow.

KHADIJA: I think I'm too hyper to glow. I probably glisten, but unfortunately I'm not glistening now because I only have a *crush* on a boy but he has yet to raise my situation to a glisten or a glow.

SHAR: Who is he?

KHADIJA: He's in the meat department.

SHAR: Of course he is.

KHADIJA: Yes, he's both tough and tender.

SHAR: And thank God you still eat meat.

KHADIJA: Yes, if I was one of those spirulina girls then I'd never have the excuse to go to his counter.

(KHADIJA *and* SHAR *smile; beat.*)

SHAR: So, obviously, Khadija, I don't want you to do anything you don't want, but I *do* think that what happened to your father is still worth talking about. Maybe not for you, which I understand—

KHADIJA: I'm trying to move on—

SHAR: I understand, and I'll protect you—but I do think that stories like yours need to be aired and those responsible held accountable. *(Quiet)* Your father was *killed*. Our country needs to acknowledge that crime.

(KHADIJAh *checks her phone.*)

SHAR: I know you have to go, but on background, can you just confirm for me what you told investigators about the day the Americans detained your father?

KHADIJA: …"On background"?

SHAR: I won't use your name. I'll just say that I spoke to a family member who now lives in America.

KHADIJA: *(Pause…then)* The Taliban had attacked the Americans' convoy a day earlier; the Americans suspected that villagers helped them, specifically my father, by allowing them to use his property to fire their mortars.

SHAR: Do you think he *did* allow the Taliban to—?

KHADIJA: First of all it is not something you *allow*. They basically do what they want. But my father was very stubborn. He didn't believe in them and so he refused, at great risk to himself.

SHAR: So he didn't?—

KHADIJA: He *didn't*. Those weapons could have been fired from *any* of the properties of the village. Besides, ours was very small—the house and a tiny yard inside a wall; ten meters by ten. It could have come from anywhere.

SHAR: Were you *there* when the Americans detained him?

KHADIJA: We were talking to a neighbor in front of our house.

SHAR: Did they say why they took him?

KHADIJA: To talk to him about the attack.

SHAR: And they—?

KHADIJA: Took him away in their truck.

SHAR: Did you ever see him again?

KHADIJA: Not until his body was found. I came over after they dug him up. To identify.

SHAR: *(Pause)* Thank you. *(Beat)* It's a very different life that you have here.

KHADIJA: Shit-sherlock, as they say.

SHAR: …Wait, *who* says that?

KHADIJA: They don't say shit-sherlock?

SHAR: Oh, yeah—no, they say, "*No* shit—Sherlock."

KHADIJA: "No shit—Sherlock." *(Pause)* Got it.

(More silence, and then SHAR, delicately, tries once more.)

SHAR: I would *really* like to be able to use your name for the article.

KHADIJA: I'm sorry, but no.

SHAR: Honestly—no one reads *Harper's* anyway.

KHADIJA: *(A smile)* I'm sorry. I need to move on.

(Lights shift; BEAU and LAURA at home. beat…then—)

LAURA: Wanna go out for dinner?

BEAU: *(Not looking up)* Why—fish night at Cracker Barrel?

LAURA: Gimme a break, Beau.

(LAURA watches BEAU as he fiddles with his phone.)

LAURA: You didn't work today?

(BEAU shakes his head)

LAUR: So what'd you do?

BEAU: Hung with Tommy.

LAURA: "Mr Productive"?

BEAU: Tommy's *highly* productive.

LAURA: No—he's just *high.*

BEAU: He's a visionary.

LAURA: He lives in his parents' basement.

BEAU: *I* live with *you.*

LAURA: Yeah but he's five years older and has a drug habit.

BEAU: It's not drugs, Mom, it's *Adderall.*

LAURA: Adderall is speed.

BEAU: Adderall is a *focus-adjuster.*

(LAURA lets it go; BEAU keeps phone-fiddling…then finally looks up)

BEAU: I think I should be be more adventurous.

LAURA: In terms of dinner?

BEAU: Everything.

LAURA: Oh. Like how?

BEAU: See the world. Beyond northern Virginia.

LAURA: Okay. Is there somewhere—?

BEAU: *Indonesia.* It sounds amazing.

LAURA: I'm sure it is. How would you go there?

BEAU: Airplane.

LAURA: In what *context*—

BEAU: Non-profit; foreign service; Marines.

LAURA: You're not joining the Marines—

BEAU: Why not?

LAURA: Because you're not—

BEAU: Fine, foreign service.

LAURA: You need a degree—

BEAU: I know that—

LAURA: And probably a master's—

BEAU: I realize that—

LAURA: Okay, I just thought we were talking about these next couple—

BEAU: I can still *visit*—

LAURA: That's true, you can visit, but that takes money—

BEAU: Which is why I have a job: I can save money for two months, then go to Indonesia—

LAURA: Fine, fair enough—good luck with that.

BEAU: *(Beat)* Why, is there some sort of reason you don't want me going overseas?

LAURA: No.

BEAU: No?

LAURA: No—I don't want you going overseas because I like seeing you and knowing you're okay and I don't particularly think one needs to go overseas in order to have an "adventurous"—

BEAU: You have to see me to know I'm okay?—

LAURA: I think the world is dangerous and screwed up *enough* that we don't need to go looking for extra portions—

BEAU: But *you* did that—

LAURA: And maybe it wasn't that great—

BEAU: And so now you're fine to have your adult son selling mice and living under the same roof for the rest of his life?—

LAURA: That's not what I'm saying, Beau. I want you to have a fulfilled life and have friends that aren't mice—or "Adderall entrepreneurs" —*believe me I want that*, I just don't think you need to go to Indonesia for "fulfillment."

BEAU: Because why?—I might end up in some sort of fucked up situation?

LAURA: …Why're you saying that?

BEAU: Saying what?

LAURA: Beau?

BEAU: Mom?

LAURA: *Beau.*

BEAU: *Mom.*

LAURA: *(Pause)* Is this—? What is this? Did you talk to that—?

BEAU: Journalist?—

LAURA: Yeah—

BEAU: No—

LAURA: No?—

BEAU: She called but I didn't talk.

LAURA: …What'd she *say*?

BEAU: She asked if you'd ever talked about what happened over there and I told her to *shove it to the dark side*. But then I was like— "Oh wait—why *hasn't* Mom actually talked about that?"

LAURA: I actually *have*—

BEAU: Not about that.

LAURA: Would you *like* me to—?

BEAU: How would I know what I'd *"like"* if I don't even know what "it" *is?* Even though I do know now because I looked it up. I mean I work at a pet store but I'm not fuckin' *"challenged"*.

LAURA: …And what'd you find?

BEAU: …Old article; from like, *Army Times*.

LAURA: Which said what?

BEAU: Described what happened. How you were there that night. How you heard the guy's screams. And how you vouched for the guys who did it.

LAURA: …Okay.

BEAU: Let's just say it definitely made me curious. About how your mind works. In fact when I showed it to Tommy, he was like, "Oh yeah, no *wonder* she's like that."

LAURA: Like what?

BEAU: I dunno—bored; sad; a *shut-in*. Which then led to me wondering why you like having me around versus letting me go see the world—

LAURA: I've never not let you—

BEAU: —and then I started thinking, "Gee, isn't it odd that my mom, who once led a pretty frickin' adventurous life, now prefers living with her son on a dead end road in the blandest northern Virginia suburb of all fucking time? Why is that? What happened to the ballsy single mom in Ray Bans who used to leave me at grandma's while she went and saved the world? Why's she now selling corporate real estate and eating T V dinners?

LAURA: ...I've never had a T V dinner in my life.

BEAU: *Organic frozen lasagna with pinto beans.*

LAURA: They're *black* beans and that's not "T V dinner"—

BEAU: It's frozen and you eat it with cheap chardonnay from, like, *Long Island.*

LAURA: What is it with you and my food—?

BEAU: You're not gonna tell me what she was talking about?

(Silence...)

LAURA: Here's what I will say, Beau. *(Pause; measured)* There are times when people—women in particular— have to protect themselves. And for women in the *military,* or military *contracting* world, there's even more need. To self-protect. It's instinctual. So this was a case where I...extracted myself from a situation. For that reason. Which I'm sure one could label as... fucked up, but which *I* believe to have been the correct response. And that's all I'd like to say.

BEAU: That's it?

LAURA: For now.

BEAU: Why?

LAURA: Because I need to think about it more.

BEAU: Even though it's been 8 years and mostly no one gives a shit—

LAURA: Yes, even though.

BEAU: You're being ridiculous.

LAURA: It's my parental prerogative, what do you want for dinner?—

BEAU: Mom—

LAURA: Beau. …Everything's fine. *(Pause)* You want some fucking lasagna?

(BEAU just looks at LAURA…)

(Lights shift, as BEAU turns and finds SHAR, on a street corner)

SHAR: I didn't think you'd call back after you told me to "shove it to the dark side."

BEAU: I, ah…guess I didn't know if you were a serious journalist.

SHAR: And you've decided I am?

BEAU: There are definitely some articles to your name. I wouldn't say they're all *thrilling,* but at least they're not, like, fuckin' *blogs.*

SHAR: Well said. Either way, I'm glad I was still in town.

BEAU: *(A nod)* So I wanna ask a question.

SHAR: Go for it.

BEAU: From what I read, my Mom didn't really do anything legally wrong in terms of that case. So I'm wondering if you think she'd end up in jail if there was actually a trial.

SHAR: Depends what kind of information she withheld. Have you two talked about—?

BEAU: I'm not here to "rat" people out—

SHAR: I understand—

BEAU: You wanna ask questions, fine, but it's not why we're—

SHAR: So why're we here? On this street corner, at three in the afternoon, as per your instructions.

BEAU: I'm just investigating, same as you.

SHAR: Okay.

BEAU: You think she did something wrong?

SHAR: I think she didn't tell the full truth, and that part of her wants to fix that but she won't unless pushed.

BEAU: Does it still *matter*?

SHAR: It does—

BEAU: Why?

SHAR: Because—

BEAU: Shouldn't we move on?—

SHAR: C'mon, Beau—

BEAU: Isn't there enough other messed up shit to worry about? Why bother with something 8 years ago in a war that barely still exists?

SHAR: …Beau. Do you think our country deals with violence well?

BEAU: I have no idea—

SHAR: I think it's fair to say we don't. We basically tend to ignore it until it's far enough in the past to slap up a plaque and call it history, at which point it repeats itself.

BEAU: That's really deep.

SHAR: *(Beat)* You know who William Calley was?

BEAU: Yes—

SHAR: *Do* you?—

BEAU: *No.*

SHAR: During the Vietnam War he oversaw the massacre of three to five hundred unarmed Vietnamese villagers.

BEAU: I'm not really into history—

SHAR: He personally killed *twenty-two* of them and watched as his men gang-raped women and shot 'em through the head.

BEAU: My Mom didn't do that—

SHAR: Who along with his men, took M16s and *slaughtered* kids, then told investigators they "feared for their safety" —same words cops use today—

BEAU: Can you drive it home?—

SHAR: You asked if it matters—

BEAU: It doesn't—

SHAR: It does. When Calley was arrested, the majority of Americans were *outraged* at how he was treated—

BEAU: So—?

SHAR: *You're right to ask questions, Beau.* It's what *I'm* doing too: Asking if someone who perhaps committed murder should hold political office. *I think it's a fair discussion.*

BEAU: *(Pause)* When's your article come out?

SHAR: Two weeks, so if you have things you wanna tell me, now's the time.

BEAU: How do I know you won't trash my Mom?—

SHAR: You don't but I won't—

BEAU: How do I know?—

SHAR: Because I'm not out to trash people, I'm into saying what happened, which I'm sure was complicated—

BEAU: You mean "fucked up"—

SHAR: No—*complicated*. Look, Beau—

BEAU: You don't think there are better ways to do this?

SHAR: Well this is the way *I* do things—

BEAU: Is it gonna lead to a trial?—

SHAR: I have no idea.

BEAU: Can I see what you're writing first?

SHAR: *(A smile)* It doesn't work that way.

BEAU: *(Pause)* Fine, then neither do I. *(He turns to go—)*

SHAR: What if you had a friend who was killed? *(He stops.)* If your *best friend* was tortured to death and the three cops who did it covered for each other. Would you not *insist* that the fourth cop who heard the torture speak up?

BEAU: …I would imagine the fourth cop believes in loyalty.

SHAR: Ask the dead guy in Afghanistan about loyalty. Ask his daughter in California. Look her in the eye and ask if she thinks loyalty makes it all okay.

BEAU: …You met his daughter?

SHAR: His daughter, his neighbors, his friends—

BEAU: What'd his daughter say?

SHAR: The point is, these are real people, not cartoons. Abdul Haroun was a *real* person and he *really* died. *And there are people who are still alive who miss him everyday.*

(SHAR *lets this sink in.*)

SHAR: Call me if you wanna talk.

(Lights shift.)

(LAURA *opposite* TAYLOR MCGINNIS, *40s, cocky but very charming*)

TAYLOR: It was good to hear your voice.

LAURA: Didn't think you would again?

TAYLOR: Well, it's been eight years; we both have lives.

LAURA: We do. How *is* your life?

TAYLOR: I have a good life. *Greensboro.* Wine bar. Can't complain.

LAURA: Actually my first time to either Carolina.

TAYLOR: You're kidding—

LAURA: I'm a Pennsylvania girl.

TAYLOR: I remember that.

LAURA: Yeah?

TAYLOR: Yep.

LAURA: *(A test)* Which *part* of Pennsylvania?

TAYLOR: Outside Philly. Merion.

LAURA: Nice.

TAYLOR: I always thought that was cool.

LAURA: *Merion?*

TAYLOR: Me gettin' to be with a "northern girl".

LAURA: Oh *please*—

TAYLOR: I'm serious—

LAURA: You're so fulla shit—

TAYLOR: Jus' sayin' the truth.

LAURA: You have a family now.

TAYLOR: Doesn't mean I don't sit up straight when I'm in the presence of a beautiful northern woman.

(LAURA *smiles, shaking her head*—)

TAYLOR: I also remember you were a basketball star.

LAURA: I never said that—

TAYLOR: They gave you a scholarship to Villanova—

LAURA: I blew my knee out freshman year—

TAYLOR: *High school* star. And now?

LAURA: Real estate. *(Not much more to say)* And you're a cop?

TAYLOR: Sheriff's deputy.

LAURA: You like it?

TAYLOR: Law an' order, baby.

LAURA: *(A smile)* You're a fool.

TAYLOR: I am indeed.

*(*LAURA *and* TAYLOR *take each other in, still feeling it…)*

TAYLOR: So what brings you down here?

LAURA: Actually came to see you.

TAYLOR: …Why?

LAURA: I wanted to talk about that night at Sanchez. There's a journalist—

TAYLOR: She called me.

LAURA: You talk to her?

TAYLOR: Nooo—

LAURA: Why not?

TAYLOR: No comment.

LAURA: But why?

TAYLOR: There's no way she writes that story fair.

LAURA: She's writing it anyway—

TAYLOR: I don't give a shit—

LAURA: People will read it—

TAYLOR: I did nothing wrong, Laura, and neither did you.

LAURA: You think?—

TAYLOR: I *know*. We were trying to *help*. We were over there handin' money out like candy, only to get *ambushed*, so hell yeah we interrogated that numbskull, then we let him go—*period*. Now if you wanna think we lied to you about what happened, after all we all went through, if you wanna rewrite history eight years later 'cause the "wars on terror didn't work" or whatever—then that's your call, but facts are facts: We were doing our jobs.

LAURA: "Just following orders."

TAYLOR: Be smarter, Laura. We were there for a *specific* mission, which was to *protect and aid people the best we could*. Now the "*macro* mission" was definitely-maybe up for question, but the micro of trying to help people—*that was valid:* Build schools, dig wells, stop the people trying to fuck all that up—that's what we did, so don't sit here with twenty/twenty and say, "Oh, look what happened to the school—they blew it up" —*It doesn't negate the fact that we BUILT the goddam' school,* which is better than folks who said, "Fuck Afghanistan it's too complicated." 'Cause *that* I don't respect.

LAURA: *(A small smile)* Good to see you haven't changed, Taylor.

TAYLOR: Why would I change?

LAURA: It *does* occasionally happen.

TAYLOR: Not if you thought it through the first time.

LAURA: You thought it through?

TAYLOR: I think *everything* through, it's why I was Delta *and* it's why I was with you.

LAURA: You were trying to alleviate my suffering?

TAYLOR: Absolutely-definitely. *(He can be a charming dude.)* Don't question yourself so much. You're a beautiful woman—

LAURA: Shut the fuck up—

TAYLOR: I'm serious—beautiful, smart, you care for people—

LAURA: You're so fulla' shit—

TAYLOR: Not about that. How's your son?

LAURA: He's good. Kind of a dick these days, not really talking to me—but good. I guess I just don't wanna lose him; to the "world."

TAYLOR: You gotta let 'em go at some point.

LAURA: I know. It's like I want him to move out, but… maybe just down the block. You said on the phone you have one too?

TAYLOR: I *do* have one too, got a six year-old son, got him at Target, cute as a fucking button.

LAURA: I bet. Named what?

TAYLOR: Kawlwani.

LAURA: *(Shit-giving)* You marry a Black woman?

TAYLOR: *Latina.*

LAURA: Oh.

TAYLOR: Although after you it was hard. "Once you go white, why put up a fight."

LAURA: *Please*—

TAYLOR: For real—

LAURA: You're telling me white women are better in bed than black women?

TAYLOR: I'm telling you they try their best.

(LAURA *shakes her head, maybe a deep blush…*)

TAYLOR: I'll tell you what, having a son's the best thing I ever done.

LAURA: Better than Delta Force?

TAYLOR: *Yes, Laura.* I know you think I'm a meathead—

LAURA: I don't—

TAYLOR: Yeah you do but I'm not, or I am but I'm a *smart* one.

LAURA: You're a smart meathead?—

TAYLOR: I'm like a nice piece of *veal.*

LAURA: That would imply you're young—

TAYLOR: Fine, I'm like a *twelve ounce Wagyu ribeye, cut to order; pasture raised.* …Having a kid put combat in perspective. Before him, I just knew I wanted to help, but with my kid, it's like, "Oh—now I get the *why*". Kids need order—and *Afghan* kids shouldn't have to live under *Sharia fuckin' law* as implemented by a buncha hillbilly Pashtun lunatics. Afghan Lives *Matter, Black* Lives Matter. Even the fucking *redneck* ones count. …An' believe me, the white cops I work with?—I' watch 'em like a hawk. Each one of them's my brother but they also know I'll put one between their eyes before I let 'em take out the wrong kid for the wrong reason. Having a son made me understand all that.

(*Beat; and then:*)

LAURA: Your *Latina* wife let you name your kid Kawlwani?

TAYLOR: She's a woman of the world.

LAURA: (*Beat*) I agree that being a parent opens your eyes to how you wanna live. But also to your regrets.

TAYLOR: Like I said, my regrets are for the things I didn't think through. I don't have 'em for what you're talking about.

LAURA: The guy died, Taylor.

TAYLOR: People were dyin' all over the place. If you came for forgiveness I ain't gonna grant it *'cause you did nothin' wrong.*

LAURA: Wait 'til your son's older. Hard as you may try, they don't all turn into superheroes.

TAYLOR: What'd *yours* turn into?

LAURA: …Not sure yet, but whatever he is, it's on me.

(TAYLOR looks at LAURA hard, not smiling.)

TAYLOR: I'm gonna ask you not to talk to that journalist.

LAURA: Or else what?

TAYLOR: It's not a threat, Laura; it's about honoring what we did there. People have *families.* They have careers and they have *lives* they're trying to slowly piece together. So I'm telling you: *Leave it alone.*

LAURA: Don't tell me what to do, Taylor.

TAYLOR: All I'm tryin' to say—

LAURA: You think Hawkins should be a *mayor?*

TAYLOR: I think it's not up to you.

LAURA: *(Strong) And I'm fucking telling you it is!*

(TAYLOR regards LAURA without smiling…)

TAYLOR: Okay, Laura.

LAURA: Good.

(Beat—neither LAURA nor TAYLOR gives—)

(Lights shift)

(BEAU opposite KHADIJA at a Starbucks counter)

BEAU: *(Beat...)* This must be really weird for you.

KHADIJA: Yeah.

BEAU: Me too.

KHADIJA: *(Pause)* You really flew all the way out here?

BEAU: I know, right? All my savings. But I was just like— *"I'm doin' it!" (Pause)* I hope it's okay? That I just sorta...showed up?

KHADIJA: How did you even know how to—?

BEAU: You're on Facebook.

KHADIJA: Yeah I know, but—

BEAU: And I knew the name of your Dad—from the *Harper's* article—so then I just started doing research.

KHADIJA: But they didn't use my name.

BEAU: Yeah, but it said that a family member lived in, umm, lived in America—

KHADIJA: So you looked for all the Afghan girls in America with my last name?

BEAU: Yeah.

KHADIJA: ...I guess that makes sense.

BEAU: And then, when I, ah, when I guessed that maybe you were his daughter, it felt very real to me.

KHADIJA: What felt real?

BEAU: ...You. *(Beat)* Why didn't you want me to come out here at first?

KHADIJA: I had no idea what you wanted.

BEAU: You thought I was a psycho?

KHADIJA: *Psycho?*

BEAU: Psychotic.

KHADIJA: Yes, I thought that.

BEAU: So what made you change your mind?

KHADIJA: …I guess I just didn't want to be impolite. … And you seemed very honest.

BEAU: *(Pause)* I really liked what you said when I first called you; about how you wanted to be the type of person who always answered your phone.

(KHADIJA *smiles a little; beat…*)

BEAU: When I read the article, all I wanted to do was hide. From my work, my friends, my computer. I wanted to, like, disappear. I'd never been through something like that before. I mean…we live really quiet lives, my Mom and I. And then to suddenly feel like you have people staring at you when you go to buy some toilet paper. It freaked me out even though I know no one reads that fucking magazine. Sorry—

KHADIJA: It's okay—

BEAU: Cool. Anyway, I stopped talking to my Mom; I didn't talk to *anyone*. …Finally I started thinking what *should* I do? How do I get around this thing? How do I…understand. …And a couple days later I started trying to contact you.

(BEAU *and* KHADIJA *stand in silence.*)

BEAU: When you read the article—?

KHADIJA: It was very upsetting.

BEAU: …For me, it made me…not like my mother. What she did; what she *didn't* do. *(Honest)* It made me ashamed, even though I love her. *(Pause)* It's really weird we're in a Starbucks. I mean, it's like the last place on earth I'd expect to meet someone like you.

KHADIJA: You think Afghan people don't drink coffee?

BEAU: You drink more tea, right?

KHADIJA: I guess.

BEAU: I try not to drink too much coffee. Gets me hyper.

KHADIJA: I have a hyper problem too.

BEAU: Seriously?

KHADIJA: I think I'm naturally that way.

BEAU: I'm not, which is why it freaks me out when I *do* get that way.

KHADIJA: Is that why you're drinking a smoothie?

BEAU: This is actually just a juice with no added sugar. It's really good for you— (*Reading from the bottle*) —"kale, wheat grass, spirulina, Jerusalem artichoke— *whaaat?*

KHADIJA: What's Jerusalem artichoke?—

BEAU: I don't know—it's some sorta artichoke I guess—

KHADIJA: I've never heard of that—

BEAU: Is that, like, offensive to you?

KHADIJA: *Artichoke?*

BEAU: Jerusalem. I mean—

KHADIJA: (*A smile*) No, that's not offensive.

BEAU: (*A dumb smile*) Cool.

KHADIJA: (*Beat*) Spirulina is good for you.

BEAU: Totally. (*Silence*) Anyway so I really just wanted to say I'm sorry. About what happened to your Dad. It's brutal. And horrible. I don't know why we do stuff like that. (*Beat*) And I didn't come out here to try and convince you that my mother's a really great woman, although I guess I do want you to know that's true as well. She *is* great. But obviously great people can do horrible things. (*Beat*) So do you like America?

KHADIJA: When I first arrived I wasn't sure. I was in this housing development in a suburb of Chattanooga,

Tennessee, and I thought, "Wow, this is…definitely not very real?" It didn't feel real. But then when I moved out here I was like, "Holy smokes, this place is *amazing*". Everything was just so…*shiny*. But that can wear off and sometimes it just becomes depressing.

BEAU: Does Afghanistan get depressing?

KHADIJA: Very very much. I mean, it's been a war zone for like a thousand years. And it hasn't been shiny for *many* many years. But it does have, and I don't mean this as an insult to your country, but it does feel very… *authentic*.

BEAU: Authentic, like—?

KHADIJA: Dust. People on scooters; doing whatever it takes to get to the next day.

BEAU: *(A nod; beat…)* I didn't think you'd be this attractive so I'm kinda freaking out. *(And then)* I mean, your Facebook pictures were good, although you only had three, but they didn't really show what it's like to be standing next to you. *(Feeling idiotic…)* My psychiatry app told me to be more honest about what I'm thinking but sometimes I think I take it too far.

(BEAU and KHADIJA stand in silence.)

BEAU: I really want my Mom to meet you. I can't tell if that's dumb of me, but I think that to have her *speak* to you…would be good. Not 'cause it would fix anything, I just think that making that kind of gesture in life is good for everyone who's alive. *(Pause)* I don't even know if she would, 'cause I—

KHADIJA: I don't want to meet your mother, Beau. I think it would make me too sad.

BEAU: You don't think it would, you know…*heal*?

(KHADIJA slowly shakes her head.)

KHADIJA: I think I prefer to just move on.

(BEAU *and* KHADIJA *stand*—)

(*Lights shift*)

(LAURA *on the phone with* SHAR, *both facing out.*)

LAURA: You're a good writer.

SHAR: …Thank you.

LAURA: Has it been well received?

SHAR: I guess. There've been some calls from T V. Hard to say. I'm not sure it'll lead to a trial.

(LAURA *half-nods. beat…*)

LAURA: My son is the best thing I have. I became a contractor to make more money, even though it meant leaving my eleven year-old with my Mom for two years. I wasn't trying to save the world, I was trying to better provide. (*Pause*) And so there's stuff that I haven't told you about that night at Sanchez, that your article should've included, that I'm more ready to talk about.

SHAR: Why now?

LAURA: Because my son's not talking to me. Because of this. And I'm losing him. Because I've realized that it's better to provide my son with the truth. Better for *him*. (*Beat*) Do *you* have kids?

SHAR: No.

LAURA: Married?

SHAR: No. Just me.

(*Beat…*)

LAURA: If I speak to you, I'd be contradicting what I told investigators, which could mean—

SHAR: You made false statements.

(LAURA *nods.*)

SHAR: I won't pretend it's an easy choice.

(As lights shift and we hear—sound of a NEWS ANCHOR's *voice)*

NEWS ANCHOR: *(V O)* The recent *Harper's* article by journalist Shar Caskins points an ominous finger not just at Hawkins, McGinnis and Billings, but at others who later remained silent about what they may have seen or heard. But now, Laura Hartig, a contractor on the post that night, has divulged previously unknown details:

(T V lights find LAURA *giving a sit-down interview to the unseen T V journalist—which we watch live-feed on a giant screen, which* BEAU *and* KHADIJA *view from separate sides of the stage.* LAURA *very steady, overcoming shame so as to go on public record—)*

LAURA: I heard screams and noises that led me to think that Mr Haroun was being punched, kicked and possibly whipped. The soldiers in question were understandably obsessed with finding who had attacked and killed their colleagues and friends; *our* friends. *All* of us likely overstepped our own moral limits.

NEWS ANCHOR: *(V O)* And in what way did you overstep?

LAURA: When I walked into the interrogation room the next day, I saw…puddles of blood on the floor. Which I didn't tell investigators because I didn't think that Mr Haroun had been killed. So I decided to keep that private.

NEWS ANCHOR: *(V O)* And yet by the time of the investigation you knew that Mr Haroun had been murdered. That didn't persuade you to tell the truth about the puddles of blood?

LAURA: My colleagues had assured me that they'd released Mr Haroun, and I believed them. I believed it possible there could be a pool of blood but not a murder.

NEWS ANCHOR: *(V O)* And yet now you feel—?

LAURA: That I should tell everything I saw and heard.

NEWS ANCHOR: *(V O)* Why *now*?

LAURA: I think I'm a different person than I was. ...I think when you wrestle with regret, it changes you; makes you wanna...live better. *(Pause)* And hopefully you do. *(She remains quietly focused on camera—)*

NEWS ANCHOR: *(V O)* And if the military reopens its investigation, and the allegations against the three men prove to be true, Ms Hartig *could* face prison for making false statements to investigators.

(Lights shift)

(BEAU and LAURA, in their house, standing in silence...)

LAURA: ...Do you wanna talk? About some of what's been going on?

BEAU: *(Shaking his head)* My friends don't watch that show. *(And then)* No one cares, Mom.

LAURA: You seem to care.

BEAU: Only 'cause I know you.

LAURA: *(Pause)* Hawkins ended his campaign; the military's reopening the case; so I guess *some* people care, even if only for the sake of appearance. *(Beat)* I realize you must be thinking that I'm not who you—

BEAU: Can I ask you why we've moved three times since you got back from over there?

(No answer)

BEAU: I mean first we leave Pennsylvania when I'm thirteen—in a good school, right near grandma—to go to frickin' *Lexington Mass*—

LAURA: I wanted to start over—

BEAU: Right, but then suddenly you need "start over again" in "Bergen County," then two years later we do it *again*—

LAURA: Beau—

BEAU: Were we starting over for *you* or for me?

LAURA: For us both—

BEAU: You sure? —'Cause it's not like we went back to Merion where I *did* have friends. We just ended up *here*. In a *cul de sac*.

LAURA: I got a job down here—

BEAU: You couldn't have got one in Pennsylvania?

LAURA: It's not that simple—

BEAU: I mean you've barely even ever had a *boyfriend*, Mom. It's like you just started phoning it—

LAURA: Are you done?

BEAU: Actually no, because it *affected* me. Not having you be honest and, and *functioning*—all because you're carrying around this giant "secret" —affected me a lot. Because look at me: I'm not who I'm supposed to be, right?! I mean let's face it—I'm a little bit of a fucking weirdo and so I think you gotta take some of the blame! For yanking me around the country all because you *hated* yourself.

LAURA: Beau, you don't understand the complexity—

BEAU: The "complexity"?—

LAURA: —of the situation—

BEAU: —the *situation* is that you covered for a bunch of dudes who killed a girl's father, and you can't live with yourself so you just keep moving around so that you don't have to look in the fuckin' mirror!

(Utter quiet)

BEAU: No answer?

LAURA: I don't wanna be yelled at.

BEAU: I think it's that you don't have anything to say.

(Very long silence…)

BEAU: You know when I was in Boston?

LAURA: With Tommy?

BEAU: Yeah.

LAURA: Yes.

BEAU: I was actually in California.

LAURA: …Why?

BEAU: I went to see this girl Khadija. We went to a Starbucks.

LAURA: Who's Khadija?

BEAU: Daughter of the guy who died.

(LAURA absorbs, floored.)

LAURA: *What?*

BEAU: Would you'd rather I'd gone on *60 Minutes*?

LAURA: No, but I—…

(Silence…)

LAURA: …What'd you say to her?

BEAU: Told her you were a good person. Although that was before I knew about the puddles.

(LAURA at a complete loss…)

BEAU: Go ahead and say something, Mom.

(Beat. LAURA looks for words…)

LAURA: …What was she like?

BEAU: She was nice.

LAURA: …And you went there…on your own?

BEAU: Yeah. *(Pause) What do you think of that?*

(BEAU turns; leaves. Silence. LAURA alone…)

(Lights shift. SHAR outside a Starbucks)

TAYLOR: Shar Caskins, right?

(SHAR turns and sees TAYLOR.)

SHAR: …Yeah.

TAYLOR: *(Hand extended)* Taylor McGinnis. You mentioned me in your *Harper's* article; and on *60 Minutes.*

SHAR: …That's right, I did.

TAYLOR: Sorry, didn't mean to sneak up on you.

SHAR: That's okay—

TAYLOR: Although I did wanna talk to you. *(A look around)* I've been to New York but never this part.

SHAR: What can I do for you, Taylor?

TAYLOR: You enjoyin' your fifteen minutes? Hawkins dropped out, the three of us maybe goin' to trial. You get some sorta staff job outta that?

(SHAR's non-answer is a yes.)

TAYLOR: Good. Big step up from freelance. No more riveting online articles about about women's college volleyball; *"housing fiascos"* in Rockland County. You can get back to the "important stuff." After all, you're pushin' forty, career had gotten sidetracked, no kids, no boyfriend; must've been a little rough.

SHAR: You done?

TAYLOR: Not quite—

SHAR: Well hurry up because I need to be somewhere—

TAYLOR: The thing with people like you is that you're
angry and you don't even know why. So you take it
out on others because you're lost. You think you know
what's right and wrong, but when it comes to actually
providing justice, you're lost. Things get grey, so it's
easier to write an article that shouts your outrage while
doing nothing. Whereas the people you're shouting
about are the ones with follow-through, who provide
for those in need rather than serving up untethered
opinion. But to you, those who put their words into
action are "predators" —or "colonial rapists"— *(A
smile)* —that was a good one. *(Pause)* The fact is you're
angry 'cause you're *useless*. So I actually feel bad for
you.

SHAR: …You don't like it when I'm angry?

TAYLOR: Doesn't get you anywhere.

SHAR: Should I not be angry 'cause it's been eight
years? Does that make me "vindictive"?

TAYLOR: Yep—

SHAR: You don't think you deserve to go to trial?—

TAYLOR: Nope—

SHAR: That something good could come from it?

TAYLOR: Just for your career.

SHAR: So you think people like you, who've essentially
admitted to torturing people, should just be allowed to
live among us like nothing ever happened?—

TAYLOR: Absolutely—

SHAR: And as a Black man, Taylor—if I may—you
really think that's fair? That you get to come home
and be all "normal" while some sixteen year-old Black
kid who robs twenty bucks at a fucking mini-mart
in Alabama, that *that* kid has to go to jail and start a

process of his whole life being fucked? You think that's
fair?

TAYLOR: We were in a war.

SHAR: Wars have rules—

TAYLOR: Sometimes they're hard to follow—

SHAR: So says the sixteen year-old Black kid—

TAYLOR: You gonna tell me about being *Black*?—

SHAR: *You're* the one who brought up "justice",
asshole—so let's talk about that, because the Afghans
you supposedly protected aren't that different from the
Black kids that the cops in this country love to shoot,
so maybe you wanna look at *your* part in all that before
you ambush me outside a fucking Starbucks. I don't
need you to put your "words into action" if action
equals bodies, be it Afghanistan or Greensboro—

TAYLOR: We didn't kill that guy—

SHAR: I never said you did—

TAYLOR: You implied it—

SHAR: I said there should be a trial—

TAYLOR: And *I* have a family, okay!?—and they don't
need to see me comin' under fire for somethin' I didn't
do!

SHAR: Is that why you're here? You want pity?

TAYLOR: Listen to me: This thing's about to become
full-on political, which is a sure way to lose the truth,
meaning my son will grow up without a Dad.

SHAR: But you think it's better for a daughter to watch
her Dad shoved into a truck and driven away not to be
seen again until his decomposed body is pulled from
some barren fucking dirt fifty feet from a sewage pit?
While meanwhile *you* come home and take your son
to Applebee's, rub him on the head and tell him how

much you love him. You wanna live in *that* country,
Taylor? —Where we send "family guys" like you
overseas to torture people? You weren't some pimply
teenager who signed up 'cause "the mill in your town
closed down." You were a professional solider in your
thirties, whose job was to *help* the Afghans, not to "gag
'em and bag 'em"—

TAYLOR: You have no idea what you're—

SHAR: Why, 'cause I'm not a soldier?—

TAYLOR: 'Cause you don't know the good we did and
you sure as shit don't know the cost!—

SHAR: My job is to *calculate* the cost! —And believe
me—I'll support the troops 'til I die but not the ones
who shout too loud about "helping the world" and
"you want me on that wall" —'cause you know
what? —We *don't* need you on that wall. Not the little
mud and brick wall in some bumfuck province of
Afghanistan! —That is NOT a wall we need a bunch of
'roid-head speed-freaks pacing up and down on—

TAYLOR: My friend's head was blown off eighteen
hours earlier—

SHAR: I understand that. I *do*. And I can only imagine.
(*Measured but strong*) But what you did was still wrong.
Because you didn't draw the line; you got to the grey
and just kept going. Which is too bad, because when
you plow through the grey, it's only more victims.
Abdul-Jalil Haroun's daughter is a victim, and she's
with us, she is *among* us, and her pain shouldn't be
ignored.

TAYLOR: How about you go fuck yourself.

SHAR: You're an eloquent dude.

TAYLOR: (*Turning back—steady*) Do you know what'll
happen if this keeps going? I will become an outcast. I
will lose my job, the respect of my son—

SHAR: Should've thought of that before—

TAYLOR: And maybe *you* should try having a family of your own. Help you figure out what's worth dying for and protecting, in terms of *all* kids—mine and the ones we were over there trying to help— Maybe you'd see the picture's bigger than—

SHAR: *Get the fuck away from me*—

TAYLOR: I'm not touching you—

SHAR: *STEP BACK! (And then) NOW!*

(TAYLOR *just stands; he is close but not touching; hard to gauge the threat…)*

TAYLOR: Fine. *(He doesn't move—as)*

(Lights shift viciously—)

(A Denny's. BEAU, KHADIJA *and* BEAU *sit in complete silence…)*

BEAU: *(…then, finally)* Are you gonna say something, Mom?

LAURA: Of course. I just…I wanna find the right words. Now that I'm here. *(Pause)* I didn't think I would feel this way.

KHADIJA: Which way?

LAURA: Like my heart has dropped into my stomach.

*(*KHADIJA *perhaps allows a polite smile; beat.)*

BEAU: *(Quiet, to* KHADIJA*)* Are you okay?

KHADIJA: Yes.

BEAU: *(To* LAURA*)* Are *you*?

*(*LAURA *smiles, nods, appreciative of his concern)*

BEAU: …Did I tell you Khadija works at the Whole Foods?

LAURA: You did.

BEAU: She's trying to put her life back together.

KHADIJA: I'm extremely lucky to be here; in a country where that's possible. As I told Beau, many of my friends and relatives would never have that chance.

LAURA: I suppose it's the least our country can do. Have you managed to make friends?

KHADIJA: The aunt of my aunt has a circle of friends who are very nice, although they're mostly older, and either Afghan or Iranian. But through them I go to weddings, and funerals, and baby showers.

BEAU: No bar mitzvahs I guess.

KHADIJA: I'm sorry?

BEAU: Sorry, it was a stupid joke.

LAURA: Beau likes to break the ice.

KHADIJA: It doesn't have to be fully icy. It can just be warm.

(*They share a smile*)

KHADIJA: I've also tried to meet people my age. People who work at the store; I take an aerobics class.

BEAU: Really?

KHADIJA: Half aerobics, half *"spin"*? Do you know spin?

BEAU: With the bikes?

KHADIJA: Yes; it's insane.

LAURA: It always seems so hard.

KHADIJA: I've never sweated so much in my life. The instructor's name is Renaldo.

LAURA: *Renaldo?*

KHADIJA: Yes.

LAURA: What is that?

KHADIJA: It's his name.

LAURA: Yes but where's he from?

KHADIJA: He's from the spin class.

BEAU: She means which country.

KHADIJA: Oh right; I don't know.

LAURA: It sounds Brazilian.

BEAU: You're just saying that 'cause of the soccer player.

LAURA: Am I?

BEAU: *Yes*, you are.

KHADIJA: …I'm not sure where he's from. But he's very insane. But he's also very cute.

BEAU: *(Quietly incredulous)* Really?

KHADIJA: *(Innocent)* What?—

BEAU: Nothing—

KHADIJA: It's just an observation—

BEAU: Are you even supposed to *talk* that way about guys?

KHADIJA: Why wouldn't I?

BEAU: 'Cause culturally you're from a place where women aren't supposed to be—

KHADIJA: Bold and outgoing?

BEAU: …*Yeah?*

KHADIJA: Anyway. *(To* LAURA*)* I'm trying to become more like *your* culture.

LAURA: Be careful what you wish for.

KHADIJA: Not *all* of your culture, just the good parts.

LAURA: I think that's cool.

BEAU: Mom, stop trying to be cool by saying "cool," it's extremely uncool.

LAURA: Okay, Beau.

(Beat…and then, LAURA *more formally addresses* KHADIJA*)*

LAURA: So first off, I want to, obviously, talk about what happened, in 2009. But even before that, I wanna *start* by saying how…*deeply*…very deeply sorry I am; for what happened to your father. For my part in it. For my colleagues' part; for the way our country has not… taken responsibility for it. It's not fair. To you, your relatives, your *father,* obviously. *(Pause)* I think about what happened…all the time. And I am extremely ashamed. Because we should've done better. And we didn't. And I'm sorry.

*(*KHADIJA *absorbs, head slightly bowed…then:)*

KHADIJA: Thank you. *(Beat)* Like I told Beau, I didn't want to meet you.

LAURA: I know.

KHAD: I'm trying to move on.

LAURA: It's understandable.

KHADIJA: *(Beat)* But now that you're here; that I meet you; may I ask you something?

LAURA: Of course.

KHADIJA: …Did you ever see my father?

LAURA: Yes. I saw him when he was brought in.

KHADIJA: What did he look like?

LAURA: I don't really know.

KHADIJA: Why not?

LAURA: There was a cloth sack over his head.

*(*BEAU *looks at* LAURA, *not having known this…)*

KHADIJA: Was that the only time you saw him?

LAURA: No. There was a moment, later that night, when I heard him yelling out in pain. And so I went over to the room to, to see what was happening. And one of the soldiers who was…interrogating him, was outside the room drinking a…a Gatorade. And I asked him what was going on and he said they were trying to get the right information out of him; out of your father. And then he suggested that *I* go in there; that maybe I could have a more, ah, subtle effect on him.

KHADIJA: …I didn't know that.

LAURA: I haven't really told anyone.

BEAU: Did you go in?

LAURA: Yes.

KHADIJA: Did you interrogate him?

LAURA: I'd describe it more as a conversation. I wasn't military, I was a contractor there to help with supplies. I wasn't there to interrogate.

KHADIJA: So what did you talk about?

LAURA: I asked about his family. His life in the village. I learned that you and he had only moved back there after your mother died. That he had grown up there, but that your family had actually lived in Kabul for a while.

KHADIJA: *(Quiet)* Yes.

BEAU: Was there a translator?

LAURA: No. *(To* KHADIJA*)* As I'm sure you know, he spoke some English. Not a lot, but…

KHADIJA: Yes.

LAURA: He seemed to be a very nice man.

BEAU: Did you think that he'd been involved in the attack the day before?

LAURA: I have no idea. I asked him once, and he said no. That he'd been in Kabul that day.

KHADIJA: Why did you stop asking him?

LAURA: Because if he *had* been involved, I don't think he would have told me. And I'm not sure it mattered anyway.

BEAU: Why?

LAURA: If I was living in that village and the Americans were running around in the way we run around, and the Taliban asked, or even *demanded* to use my property, I might've said yes too. So I wasn't sure it mattered.

BEAU: Do you think the Special Forces guys thought that too?

LAURA: Maybe in the back of their minds, but in the front of their minds, they thought they could get that information from him.

BEAU: Are you gonna tell the investigators all that?

LAURA: I will. *(To* KHADIJA*)* I'm meeting with them next week; and I'm willing to accept whatever punishment they give me. *(Beat; to* KHADIJA*)* I want to say something about what your father said that night, when I asked him about his life. *(Pause)* He said he had only one daughter and that he loved her like she was the most important thing in the entire world. That his two sons had died, and his wife had died, and that you were his precious jewel. He said you were like *lapis.* The blue stone? I'm sure you know this.

*(*KHADIJA *nods)*

LAURA: He carried one in his pocket, tiny but incredibly blue. I guess Afghanistan is famous for it?

*(*KHADIJA *nods.)*

LAURA: And then…I won't forget this…he said that
he believed you were six thousand years old, just
like the lapis, plucked from a cave in the Hindu Kush
Mountains. And that he was sure that no matter what
happened, you would somehow survive for *another* six
thousand years. That that is how unique you are.

(Beat)

KHADIJA: It's true he used to compare me to lapis.
(Pause) But I never heard that last part.

LAURA: I should have helped him more. …I don't
expect you to forgive me. But I wanted to meet you.
Which I thank Beau for making happen; I wouldn't
have had the courage to be here without him. *(Beat)* I
can't fix what I broke. *(Pause)* I can only sit before you
and…simply sit before you.

*(KHADIJAh looks at LAURA, a small smile of appreciation
upon her face.)*

KHADIJA: *(Quiet)* Thank you.

(LAURA maybe nods; silence…)

(Lights shift)

*(Music lands on the stage. A moment passes. The actors
switch positions. The backdrop opens and transitions into
something bigger…a backdrop of emptiness and brick and
depth. Finally the music fades save for the echo of a single
note that lasts throughout the following:)*

(As KHADIJA stands in light and speaks to us:)

KHADIJA: I am standing in La Jolla California. *(Pause)*
My God I love it here. It's like a T V show. With green
patio furniture and bright blue S U Vs and swimming
pools warmer than coffee. And right now, on this
quiet Friday night, it's like I don't ever want to leave,
because there's so much to take in and I want to
remember it all. …The air with no dust. As though

every resident had vigorously wiped their feet before stepping into town. ...The light that literally shimmers; fragile but proud as it fades beyond our cliffs. *(Pause)* And of course my beloved Whole Foods. ...From its parking lot I watch the families go by: Mothers and daughters, fathers and sons. So many people *responsible for one another. (Pause)* I see a mother and her son. I see the love that they have; the loyalty and truth. The lengths to which they would go, as they walk across the parking lot, searching out their future on this perfect-temperature night. ...They deserve to have each other. *(Pause)* Their desire to survive is just as strong as mine.

(Lights shift)

(KHADIJA *turns to find* BEAU *standing there; beat.)*

BEAU: Hey.

KHADIJA: Hey.

BEAU: You okay?

KHADIJA: Yes. *(Pause)* Did your mother leave?

BEAU: Yeah, she had to get back for work. I was thinking I might stay a couple more days. Not that you should have to entertain me or anything, I just...I wanted to see San Diego.

(KHADIJA *nods, maybe a smile; beat.)*

BEAU: You okay?

KHADIJA: Yes, and you?

BEAU: Yeah, really good. ...Thank you for meeting with my Mom. It meant a lot to her. I know it meant a lot to me.

KHADIJA: It was good it happened. *(Pause)* But I also think we should talk about what happened.

BEAU: Okay. *(Pause)* Why, what happened?

KHADIJA: *(Beat)* You are very honest, Beau. …And I would like to be very honest with you. *(Beat…)* It was the Taliban.

BEAU: …What about them?

KHADIJA: They were the ones.

BEAU: …What?

KHADIJA: *(Pause)* It was the Taliban who killed my father, not the Americans.

BEAU: …Why are you saying that?

KHADIJA: Because it's true. He was released by the Americans, but before he could come home, the Taliban found him and they took him away and beat him until he died; then they buried him but no one knew until the grave was discovered.

BEAU: …How do you know this?

KHADIJA: One of our neighbors saw him being taken by them.

BEAU: And you've known this the whole time?

KHADIJA: I learned it soon after they found him.

BEAU: But…why would the Taliban kill someone who'd been accused of helping them?

KHADIJA: I think because he had been detained by the Americans, and the Taliban assumed he had collaborated.

BEAU: How?

KHADIJA: By becoming an informant.

BEAU: But *had* he?

KHADIJA: I think the Taliban was just trying to send a message to our village.

(BEAU tries to absorb all this, almost daze-like.)

BEAU: And no one told the American investigators any of this?

KHADIJA: No.

BEAU: *Why not?!*

KHADIJA: By this time, people disliked the Americans more than they disliked the Taliban.

BEAU: So they just let the Americans take the blame?

KHADIJA: It seems that the Americans knew how to handle the blame. They just let it slip from their shoulders.

BEAU: Not my Mom! I mean, what do you think she just *went* through?

KHADIJA: I agree. It was incredible. But it took her eight years. *(Quieter)* I think she's a good person; but the fact doesn't change that she let them beat my father and did nothing about it.

BEAU: But your father *survived*. They *released* him—

KHADIJA: The Americans still beat him—

BEAU: They interrogated him for a *night*—

KHADIJA: They beat him for no reason until there were pools of blood on the floor. And yes, he survived, but the moment they let him go he was as good as dead.

BEAU: *Why the fuck didn't you say all this before?!*

KHADIJA: I told you I didn't want to meet her. And even then she was still right to apologize. As far as she knows, they *did* kill my father.

BEAU: But it's not what *happened*, Khadijah! It's not the *facts.* You could've told the truth and she still would've apologized without having to now maybe go to *jail!* I mean—you didn't have to fuckin' *hide* shit!

KHADIJA: *(Quiet…)* I *did* have to.

BEAU: Why?!

KHADIJA: Because otherwise they would send me back; or to jail; or both.

BEAU: Why? *(No answer)* Khadija.

KHADIJA: …Because the Taliban *did* use our property. *(She looks at him, very simply, very honestly…)* And if people knew that, I don't think they'd let me work at Whole Foods. Or live in La Jolla. Or even Chattanooga. *(She tries to smile at this feeble attempt at humor, but can't…)*

BEAU: Your father gave them permission?

KHADIJA: You have no idea what it's like there.

BEAU: What do you mean?

KHADIJA: There is no permission.

BEAU: Okay, but—

KHADIJA: There is none.

BEAU: …So they just…*took* it from him?

KHADIJA: They took it from me. *(Pause)* They took it from me.

BEAU: …But—

KHADIJA: I had no choice. They would've hurt me. Or worse. My father had *already* said no to them, which had made them very mad. So when he traveled to Kabul for a day, they came to our house.

BEAU: …It was *you*?

KHADIJA: They told me that if I didn't do what they said, that I would regret it for the rest of my life. *I was sixteen years old.*

BEAU: But couldn't you have just told investigators that it was your *father* who was forced to let them use your property?

KHADIJA: It only would have led them back to me. They would have lifted every stone.

(BEAU *looks at* KHADIJA.)

KHADIJA: I had to *live* there. It was my home. If I had said what I knew, I *too* would have been seen as a collaborator.

(*Silence;* BEAU *stands; broken*)

KHADIJA: I need you to know the situation, Beau. The Americans had killed my mother. Accidentally, but *casually.*

BEAU: But didn't they give you money?—

KHADIJA: Yes, they gave me ten thousand dollars. But it was my *mother.* …I am telling you this because what you did by getting your mother to speak to me, and what she *said*, made me not want to see her punished, because it wouldn't be fair. I shouldn't be free if it means someone else goes to prison, so I'm saying the truth, but hoping it brings us *closer* instead of further apart.

BEAU: *How?*

KHADIJA: …If your mother testifies about just the torture—then maybe that's enough. The men will be disciplined for that, and the rest will go away.

BEAU: …You want her to lie? About what you just told me—?

KHADIJA: A lie of silence. The military will never find soldiers guilty of a murder for which there is no proof. So they'll only be punished for the torture.

(BEAU *absorbs.*)

KHADIJA: This way we can all move on. (*Quiet but strong*) Because I'm not going back. I have come too far, and lost too many people along the way. I am owed my right to be here.

BEAU: *Owed?*

KHADIJA: Yes—

BEAU: But you, you *knowingly* contributed to people dying—

KHADIJA: *I didn't have a choice.* You would've done the same thing.

BEAU: ...I'm not sure.

KHADIJA: *Ask your mother.* She knows what one does to survive. And believe me, she had more choice than I. *(Pause; steady)* They will kill me if I am sent back. Knowing what I know. Having lived *here?* They will kill me.

(BEAU *just looks at* KHADIJA...)

(Lights shift)

(LAURA *turns and finds* BEAU *standing opposite...*)

LAURA: *(Beat; careful)* Are you sure?

BEAU: It's exactly what she said.

LAURA: So his death—?

BEAU: Isn't your fault.

LAURA: *(Pause)* But he *did* die?

BEAU: Yes.

LAURA: Because of the interrogation.

BEAU: ...Yes.

LAURA: *(Pause)* ...And so *what* is she saying we should we do?

BEAU: That you should testify about the torture and nothing else. So that the soldiers go to jail for just that.

(Long silence...)

LAURA: I don't think that's right.

BEAU: It's a good idea, Mom—

LAURA: It's not. If I do that, they'll keep the case open and it'll eventually lead to Khadija. C I D will go to every length to exonerate American soldiers.

BEAU: …So then what are you—?

LAURA: I think I shouldn't say another word. Just stop talking altogether. That way they'll be forced to close the case, and Khadija will be left alone.

BEAU: But wouldn't they make you testify based on what you already said?—

LAURA: I'll refuse.

BEAU: They'll put you in prison—

LAURA: Maybe, but better me than her.

BEAU: You can't just do that, Mom—

LAURA: *(Steady)* If their only witness refuses to testify, they'll close the case—

BEAU: Yeah, but *you'll* go to jail for, like, contempt—

LAURA: Think about the other option: *They will revoke Khadija's visa—*

BEAU: And *you'll* be in prison for refusing to talk about what you already talked about!—

LAURA: All I mentioned was the puddles of blood; if I retract that, they won't have enough to go on. It's not your decision, Beau.

BEAU: But she told *me;* she didn't tell *you.*

LAURA: And now *you've* told me, and I'm the one who it'll affect.

(Silence…)

LAURA: *(Quiet)* Beau? *(Pause)* You don't think Khadija deserves better than what would happen to her if this comes out? They'd *deport* her.

BEAU: She helped kill people, even if she didn't want to.

LAURA: So did I. I was over there for two years. I was helping every day. *(Beat)* If someone's going to pay the price, it should be me.

(BEAU absorbs…)

BEAU: *(Near whisper)* …That's not fair, Mom…

(LAURA regards BEAU, seeing how deep it goes…)

LAURA: Sweetheart.

(BEAU doesn't answer. she quietly goes to him and tries to hug him. He steps away. She gently tries again; he lets her half-hug him for a moment…and then he steps away; beat.)

BEAU: You're manipulating shit. *(He leaves—)*

(As lights shift. BEAU alone in a shiny new office. A long moment passes as he just stands there, deep in thought. Then, finally, SHAR enters.)

BEAU: Hi.

SHAR: *(A moment)* Hi, Beau. What're you—? Why're you here?

BEAU: I was wondering if we could talk.

SHAR: …Sure. What brings you to New York?

BEAU: The bus.

(SHAR nods…)

BEAU: Nice office.

SHAR: Thank you.

BEAU: New?

SHAR: I share it.

(Beat)

BEAU: You got something wrong, in your story about my Mom.

SHAR: Did I?

BEAU: Really wrong. But this has to be off the record. You can't use my name.

SHAR: What do you know?

BEAU: The Afghan guy wasn't killed by the Americans; he was killed by the Taliban 'cause they thought he was an informant. Which means you messed up and you need to fix it.

SHAR: …Why do you think that—?

BEAU: I just told you I can't tell you—

SHAR: Did your Mom—?

BEAU: It wasn't my Mom but that's all I'm gonna say. *You're* the one who needs to write an article saying my Mom wasn't a part of a murder—

SHAR: I can't without proof—

BEAU: Then *research* it—

SHAR: So tell me where to start— 'cause I'm not actually writing this story anymore.

BEAU: *(Quieter…)* Don't you realize what you've done? You opened up this thing and now a lotta people are hurting. I mean, don't you even care about the people you write about?

SHAR: I do—

BEAU: So then you need to re-do it and find out what really happened.

SHAR: So tell me how—

BEAU: It's not my job.

SHAR: Did you talk to people in Afghanistan?—

BEAU: No.

SHAR: *(Beat…)* …Was it Khadija? Who you spoke to?

BEAU: ...I don't know who that is.

(Beat; SHAR *tries a new tack...)*

SHAR: Beau. *(Pause)* When I was fifteen, my parents, took me to visit the Vietnamese orphanage where they'd found me.

BEAU: Enough with the stories—

SHAR: *Listen* to me. ...I saw a girl there, exactly my age but...completely *ravaged.* Her life had been stolen. And I knew that her *pain*...had somehow been meant for me. *(Pause)* Which made me wanna live correctly. For her. It's why I chose this profession. To *always* speak the truth. *(Beat; quietly forceful)* We all need to speak the truth, Beau.

(Real silence)

SHAR: What did Khadija say?

(Beat; no answer)

SHAR: We need to do this correctly. I need to fix what I got wrong. Otherwise your mother—and those three soldiers—are very likely looking at prison. *(Beat)* What'd she tell you?

BEAU: *(Very quiet)* ...I don't know what you're talking about.

SHAR: ...I can just ask her myself. ...I can tell her what you're telling me and see how she reacts. *(Pause)* Beau? It's not better the other way. You said it yourself.

(Very long beat)

BEAU: *(Near whisper)* ...She said someone in the village saw her father being taken away.

SHAR: ...Did she say who?

*(*BEAU *shakes his head.)*

SHAR: Did she say if her father had allowed the Taliban to use their property?

BEAU: Yeah. She said he did.

SHAR: *(Pause)* But Beau. He was in Kabul that day. I verified it. So he couldn't have been the one. Which means one of you is lying.

(Painstaking silence)

SHAR: Beau?

(More silence…)

BEAU: *(Pause…a whisper)* …She said she had.

(SHAR *stands, barely able to believe it.* BEAU *looks up at her…)*

BEAU: They would've killed her.

(Silence as SHAR *just looks at* BEAU.)

BEAU: You can't use her name.

SHAR: …It's my job.

BEAU: *(Near whisper)* But I'm asking you. *(No answer)* Please? *(Beat; barely audible)* Please?

(SHAR *watches* BEAU…)

SHAR: I'll need to name you as a source.

(BEAU *looks at* SHAR.)

BEAU: But people will suffer.

SHAR: Yes. And we will all have to live with that. But it's the right thing to do.

(BEAU *doesn't answer. Beat)*

(Lights shift; BEAU *and* LAURA. *Silence. And then—)*

LAURA: I'm meeting with investigators this afternoon.

BEAU: …I thought it was Friday.

LAURA: No. Today.

BEAU: …What're you gonna say?

LAURA: That I'm not willing to testify because I don't want to self-incriminate.

BEAU: ...But then won't they definitely charge you for—?

LAURA: Yes.

(Beat)

BEAU: Did you know that that journalist is poking around?

LAURA: ...What do you mean?

BEAU: I heard she's still investigating.

LAURA: How? *(No answer)* Who'd you hear that from, Beau?

BEAU: ...She called me.

LAURA: Why would she call *you?*

BEAU: To ask questions.

LAURA: Like what?

BEAU: ...Like about what happened. I think she'd had contact with some of the people in Khadija's village.

LAURA: ...Beau?

BEAU: What?

LAURA: Is that really true?

BEAU: Yeah.

LAURA: And what were the villagers telling her?

BEAU: Something about...you know, the stuff we were talking about.

LAURA: ...What'd you tell her?

BEAU: Nothing.

LAURA: Beau?

(No answer...)

LAURA: *Beau?*—

BEAU: Nothing. She asked me questions and then asked me to confirm if I thought they were true.

LAURA: And you said—?

BEAU: Nothing!

(LAURA *looks at* BEAU, *knowing he's lying*)

LAURA: Did she call you or did you call her?

BEAU: ...I saw her.

LAURA: In person?

BEAU: Yeah.

LAURA: ...Oh Jesus.

BEAU: What?

LAURA: What have you done, Beau?

BEAU: *(Beat; trying to own it)* I told the truth.

LAURA: About what Khadija told you?

BEAU: Yes. About what she did.

LAURA: And did Shar say what she was gonna do?

BEAU: She said she was gonna write about it. She said she *had* to. Even though I asked her not to.

(BEAU *is trying hard to own the correctness of what he did; but it's hard.* LAURA *looks for words...*)

LAURA: I want you to listen very close to me, Beau—

BEAU: I don't wanna do that—

LAURA: *Listen to me!*

(BEAU *waits;* LAURA *attempts to compose herself and her thoughts...which come slowly at first*)

LAURA: I understand that you think I haven't been a good example for you. And I know I may have...held you too tight; and kept you too close. And that may have screwed you up. But I never lied to you, Beau—

BEAU: *Of course you fucking lied!*—

LAURA: No—what I did was *omit*. Which I now know was a mistake. But it was because I wanted you to know a better version of me.

BEAU: *It didn't work*—

LAURA: I agree. In fact it probably did the opposite. … But you're your own person now, Beau. No matter how tight I've held you. Which means there is *NO excuse* for what you've just done. You have fucked with another person's fate.

BEAU: Is that what you think?—

LAURA: *Very much!* And it will be you who has to live with that. It will be entirely on *you!*—

BEAU: I've been asking for the same thing you had done, Mom: *omission!*—

LAURA: It's *not* the same!—

BEAU: It i*s!* You chose not to tell me things for 8 years, and so I was asking *you* not to say things so that she wouldn't get in trouble and *you* wouldn't go to prison!—

LAURA: But it wasn't your call, it was *mine!* What *you* need to do is take care of yourself and *be a fucking man!!*—

BEAU: *I WAS, MOM! —I HAD A SOLUTION!*—

LAURA: *But it wasn't a good plan, Beau!* It wouldn't have worked!

BEAU: *How do YOU know?!*—

LAURA: *Because it wasn't realistic!!* And because it was as much about *YOU as it was about Khadija or me.* It was

about *you* needing to be here! With me! *(Pause; quieter)*
But that has to be over now.

(BEAU *absorbs for a long beat… then, calm but very*
strong—)

BEAU: Fine. Then I'll leave. And I hope I never fucking
see you again.

(BEAU *leaves—as lights shift—)*

(LAURA *turns and speaks to us, declarative and honest; a*
testimonial; the need to confess overriding all self-pity)

LAURA: Khadijah's father didn't tell me he thought
she would live for six thousand years. I made that up.
(Pause) He did tell me *about* her; for a second; said she
reminded him of lapis; but said nothing about her
surviving thousands of years. What he *did* do…was
beg me for his life. Told me he had a daughter, then
begged me to stop the soldiers from beating him to
death. *(Pause)* They were on a beating "break" when I
spoke to him, and he literally raised himself onto his
bleeding knees and *begged* me to make them stop. *(Beat)*
I wake up, often, wondering why I didn't. Barely even
tried. For an instant maybe. When I exited the room
and Taylor was, there finishing his blue Gatorade, I
said to him, "Don't you think he's had enough?" And
Taylor looked at me, with that look when someone
knows they kinda own you even if they don't. And
he said, "Let us take care of it, Laura. We know what
we're doing." And I said…okay. *(Beat)* What is up
with someone who walks away from that? …I used to
think of myself as empathetic. But at that moment…
in that moment, I just let it fall away. My humanity, I
guess. Just let it utterly dissipate. *(Beat)* And then…I
thought of something else. Of *my* kid. Beau. And I
thought, "I will always try to make him proud. Unlike
what this Afghan guy in the other room has done
for *his* kid." *"I'll* never collaborate in an effort to kill

people trying to help me." *"I'll* never risk my kid's
life in order to aid and abet evil." ...I actually thought
that. *(Beat)* And then, eight years later, I sit there with
this man's daughter, in a fucking Denny's in southern
California, and I tell her that her father thinks she'll
live for thousands of years. As if that "gesture;" that
lie...will somehow restore to her the life that I stood
and watched robbed. ...As if *words* could *ever* make up
for *death. (Pause)* How am I supposed to live with that?
How is *she? (Beat...)* It just seems God should throw
His hands up in disgust. *(Beat)* I'm so bad. *(Beat...)* I'm
so fucking bad.

(Lights shift)

(And...music...as KHADIJA *appears in a yellow
Immigration and Customs Enforcement jumpsuit.)*

(Lights shift again to find KHADIJA *and* LAURA *on the
phone.)*

LAURA: Khadija? *(Pause)* It's Laura.

KHADIJA: ...Hello.

LAURA: I wanted to...to say how sorry I am. *(No
answer)* I understand how upset you must be; I can
only imagine. But I think there's still a way to fix this.
To argue that you deserve to stay, based on the fact
that you didn't have a choice—

KHADIJA: The authorities here have already made their
decision.

LAURA: ...And—?

KHADIJA: I'm being sent back.

LAURA: ...To—?

KHADIJA: Afghanistan.

LAURA: ...You know that for sure?

KHADIJA: I don't think they would joke.

LAURA: But they said on the phone it was still—

KHADIJA: They told me this morning.

LAURA: *(Absorbing)* …Jesus.

KHADIJA: …I would rather prison.

LAURA: *(Pause)* Do you have family you can contact? Back home?

KHADIJA: They won't accept me. They will consider me…tarnished. *(Beat; then, steady)* I don't understand the reporter. It is the *soldiers* who should be punished. For what I did I had no choice.

LAURA: But that's not how people see it.

KHADIJA: But it's the truth.

LAURA: I know—

KHADIJA: So then why can't I stay? Because I was forced to let some uneducated freaks use my father's house back in Afghanistan? That if I "conspired" against this country once—?

LAURA: …You might do it again.

KHADIJA: *(Neutral)* I work at fucking Whole Foods. *(Silence)* Is there something that you want from me? Why you called?

LAURA: No.

KHADIJA: *(Beat…)* I do not mean this against *you*, Laura. But this is what makes people hate.

LAURA: …I understand.

KHADIJA: I don't think you actually do. *(Beat…)* And your son?

LAURA: He left.

KHADIJA: …To where?

LAURA: I don't know. He just…he went away.

KHADIJA: For good?

LAURA: Maybe.

KHADIJA: …I see. *(Beat…)* I should hang up. Other people need the phone.

LAURA: Okay. *(Pause)* Maybe I can try to contact you? Once you're back in your country?

KHADIJA: I don't think so.

LAURA: …Okay.

KHADIJA: *(Pause)* Goodbye, Laura.

LAURA: Goodbye, Khadija.

(Silence…and then music quietly descends…as lights slowly cross-fade to find BEAU, KHADIJA, SHAR *and* TAYLOR, *all upstage…)*

*(*LAURA *stands alone downstage……)*

(The following is very simple, to us)

SHAR: In twenty years, no one will care.

LAURA: About a day in 2009 when some American named "Laura" returned to her bunk and read a back issue of *Vanity Fair* while the Special Forces guy she'd been fucking beat the shit out of a man named Haroun. *(Pause)* Beau was right about that.

BEAU: No one will even remember.

LAURA: An overzealous text book will have reclassified our entire war there as victory.

TAYLOR: We will try to move on. Putting the pieces back together. For better or worse. And the rest of it will fade.

LAURA: Until eventually no one cares. *(Beat)* Except for a few. Standing like broken toys; cracked and frozen; wondering what we've done.

KHADIJA: …This is what it feels like.

LAURA: …We are right here.

KHADIJA: ……We are all right here.

(Lights slowly fade on all five characters staring out…)

END OF PLAY

www.ingramcontent.com/pod-product-compliance
Lightning Source LLC
Chambersburg PA
CBHW052214090426
42741CB00010B/2535